quick and simple recipes
mediterranean

Contents

Mediterranean Ingredients

ANCHOVIES These come in several forms. Anchovies can be treated almost as a seasoning in many recipes. Salted anchovies are sold in bottles and must be rinsed thoroughly to remove the excess salt. If the anchovies are whole, remove the heads and bones before using. If they are preserved in oil, remove them from the oil and drain them on absorbent kitchen paper. Some recipes require that anchovies are soaked in milk for 10–15 minutes (this makes the fillets less salty and less oily). By doing so the anchovies will simply melt on cooking. Do not soak the anchovies in milk if the fillets are to be used uncooked as in salads, for example.

CANNED TOMATOES As the British climate does not produce an abundance of outdoor grown, sun-ripened tomatoes, good-quality, tinned Italian plum tomatoes are the next best thing for making sauces. The fruit should be deep red and the liquid should be thick and not watery. Buy them whole or chopped.

CAPERS The flower buds of a bush native to the Mediterranean, capers are available both salted and preserved in vinegar. Small capers generally have a better flavour than larger ones. When using salted capers, it is important to soak and rinse them to remove the excess salt. Those preserved in vinegar should be drained and rinsed before use.

DRIED HERBS These days, most recipes call for fresh herbs but dried herbs still have their place. Oregano dries particularly well and has a much less astringent flavour when dried; it is essential in tomato sauces. Other herbs that dry well are rosemary, sage and thyme. Dried basil, however, is no substitute for fresh.

DRIED MUSHROOMS The most commonly available – and most affordable – type of dried mushroom is porcini. They are usually sold in 10 g packets which is generally plenty for one or two recipes and should be soaked in almost boiling water or stock for 20–30 minutes, until tender. Carefully squeeze out any excess liquid – it will still be hot – and then chop as needed. Reserve the liquor as it contains a great deal of flavour. It is wise, however, to strain it before use as it can contain grit.

DRIED PULSES Pulses are an excellent source of carbohydrate and also contain protein, making them particularly useful to vegetarians. Dried pulses should all be treated in the same way – soak them overnight in plenty of water (2 to 3 times their volume), then drain and cover with fresh water. Bring to the boil and boil hard for 10 minutes, reduce the temperature and simmer gently, until tender (check packet instructions for full cooking times). Do not add salt to dried pulses until they are cooked as salt will make the skins tough. Mediterranean cooking makes use of a large number of different types of pulses and lentils.

CANNELLINI BEANS These beans are long and slender with a creamy texture. Cannellini beans take up other flavours very well, especially garlic, herbs and olive oil.

BORLOTTI BEANS These are large, rounded beans which cook to a uniform brown colour. They also have a creamy texture and are very good in soups and stews.

BROAD BEANS These are available dried; either whole, with skins or split. The whole ones are excellent in soups. The split beans are popular in Eastern European countries, as well as Greece and Turkey where they are used in dishes such as falafel.

CHICKPEAS Chickpeas were introduced from the Middle East. Look out for big ones when buying them dry. They are excellent in soups and also in vegetable dishes. Dried chickpeas need a long cooking time, but you can use tinned ones in their place.

LENTILS Look for Lentilles de Puy, possibly the best flavoured of the lentil family. They are small and beautifully coloured from green-brown to blue. They also hold their shape well when cooked, making them easy to serve as a side dish – simply dress with olive oil. Similar lentils named Castelluccio are also grown in Umbria. They are also small but paler green in colour. Lentils are traditionally served with Bollito Misto, a famous New Year's Eve dish consisting of various meats, lentils and mostarda di cremona (see below).

FLOUR In most Mediterranean recipes where flour is required, plain flour can easily be substituted. However, when making pizza or pasta dough, look for Tipo 'oo' flour which is very fine and very strong, making it ideal for these two dishes. If you cannot find it, use strong bread flour instead.

MOSTARDA DI CREMONA Also known as mostarda di frutta, it is made of candied fruits such as peaches, apricots, pears, figs and cherries which are preserved in a honey, white wine and mustard syrup. It is available from large supermarkets and specialist shops.

OLIVES Olives grow all over the Mediterranean and are synonymous with Mediterranean cooking. Olives are available in most supermarkets, although it is worth looking for them in specialist shops that might preserve them with more interesting flavours. If you are lucky enough to find fresh olives, soak them in a very strong brine for a couple of weeks, then rinse them and preserve in oil and flavourings of your choice.

SUN-DRIED TOMATOES Although they seem ubiquitous now, sun-dried tomatoes were unavailable outside Italy until the end of the 1980s. Sun-dried tomatoes are ripe plum tomatoes which have been dried in the sun. Often they have been rehydrated by being soaked in water and then preserved in oil. To use them, simply drain them on absorbent kitchen paper and chop as necessary. Also available now are semi-dried tomatoes, which have a sweeter, fresher flavour and a softer, less leathery texture. If you find sun-dried tomatoes which are not in oil, put them into a bowl and cover with boiling water. Leave for about 30 minutes, or until softened, before using.

Chicken Basquaise

Ingredients
Serves 4–6

1.4 kg/3 lb chicken, cut into 8 pieces
2 tbsp plain flour
salt and freshly ground black pepper
3 tbsp olive oil
1 large onion, peeled and sliced
2 red peppers, deseeded and cut into thick strips
2 garlic cloves, peeled and crushed
150 g/5 oz spicy chorizo sausage cut into 1 cm/½ inch pieces
200 g/7 oz long-grain white rice
450 ml/¾ pint chicken stock
1 tsp crushed dried chillies
½ tsp dried thyme
1 tbsp tomato purée
125 g/4 oz Spanish air-dried ham, diced
12 black olives
2 tbsp freshly chopped parsley

1 Dry the chicken pieces well with absorbent kitchen paper. Put the flour in a polythene bag, season with salt and pepper and add the chicken pieces. Twist the bag to seal, then shake to coat the chicken pieces thoroughly.

2 Heat 2 tablespoons of the oil in a large heavy-based saucepan over a medium-high heat. Add the chicken pieces and cook for about 15 minutes, turning on all sides, until well browned. Using a slotted spoon, transfer to a plate.

3 Add the remaining olive oil to the saucepan, then add the onion and peppers. Reduce the heat to medium and cook, stirring frequently, until starting to colour and soften. Stir in the garlic and chorizo and continue to cook for a further 3 minutes. Add the rice and cook for about 2 minutes, stirring to coat with the oil, until the rice is translucent and golden.

4 Stir in the stock, crushed chillies, thyme, tomato purée and salt and pepper and bring to the boil. Return the chicken to the saucepan, pressing gently into the rice. Cover and cook over a very low heat for about 45 minutes until the chicken and rice are cooked and tender.

5 Gently stir in the ham, black olives and half the parsley. Cover and heat for a further 5 minutes. Sprinkle with the remaining parsley and serve immediately.

Chicken Cacciatore

Ingredients

Serves 4

2–3 tbsp olive oil
125 g/4 oz pancetta or
    streaky bacon, diced
25 g/1 oz plain flour
salt and freshly ground
    black pepper
1.4–1.6 kg/3–3½ lb
    chicken, cut into
    8 pieces
2 garlic cloves, peeled
    and chopped
125 ml/4 fl oz red wine
400 g can chopped
    tomatoes
150 ml/¼ pint chicken
    stock
12 shallots, peeled
1 bay leaf
1 tsp brown sugar
1 tsp dried oregano
1 green pepper, deseeded
    and chopped
225 g/8 oz chestnut or
    field mushrooms,
    thickly sliced
2 tbsp freshly chopped
    parsley
freshly cooked
    tagliatelle, to serve

CHEF'S TIP
Use chestnut or field
mushrooms in this recipe
because they have a
strong flavour and will
also help to add colour to
the sauce.

1 Heat 1 tablespoon of the olive oil in a large, deep frying pan and add the diced pancetta or bacon and stir-fry for 2–3 minutes, or until crisp and golden brown. Using a slotted spoon, transfer the pancetta or bacon to a plate and reserve.

2 Season the flour with salt and pepper, then use to coat the chicken. Heat the remaining oil in the pan and brown the chicken pieces on all sides for about 15 minutes. Remove from the pan and add to the bacon.

3 Stir the garlic into the pan and cook for about 30 seconds. Add the red wine and cook, stirring and scraping any browned bits from the base of the pan. Allow the wine to boil until it is reduced by half. Add the tomatoes, stock, shallots, bay leaf, brown sugar and oregano and stir well. Season to taste.

4 Return the chicken and bacon to the pan and bring to the boil. Cover and simmer for 30 minutes, then stir in the peppers and mushrooms and simmer for a further 15–20 minutes, or until the chicken and vegetables are tender and the sauce is reduced and slightly thickened. Stir in the chopped parsley and serve immediately with freshly cooked tagliatelle.

Fried Whitebait with Rocket Salad

Ingredients
Serves 4

450 g/1 lb whitebait, fresh or frozen
oil, for frying
85 g/3 oz plain flour
½ tsp of cayenne pepper
salt and freshly ground black pepper

For the salad

125 g/4 oz rocket leaves
125 g/4 oz cherry tomatoes, halved
75 g/3 oz cucumber, cut into dice
3 tbsp olive oil
1 tbsp fresh lemon juice
½ tsp Dijon mustard
½ tsp caster sugar

1 If the whitebait are frozen, thaw completely, then wipe dry with absorbent kitchen paper.

2 Start to heat the oil in a deep-fat fryer. Arrange the fish in a large, shallow dish and toss well in the flour, cayenne pepper and salt and pepper.

3 Deep-fry the fish in batches for 2–3 minutes, or until crisp and golden. Keep the cooked fish warm while deep-frying the remaining fish.

4 Meanwhile, to make the salad, arrange the rocket leaves, cherry tomatoes and cucumber on individual serving dishes. Whisk the olive oil and the remaining ingredients together and season lightly. Drizzle the dressing over the salad and serve with the whitebait.

CHEF'S TIP
For an alternative salad, mix together some baby spinach, cooled, cooked petit pois and chopped spring onions, then pour over 2 tablespoons of garlic olive oil.

Italian Bean Soup

Ingredients
Serves 4

2 tsp olive oil

1 leek, washed and chopped

1 garlic clove, peeled and crushed

2 tsp dried oregano

75 g/3 oz green beans, trimmed and cut into bite-size pieces

410 g can cannellini beans, drained and rinsed

75 g/3 oz small pasta shapes

1 litre/1¼ pint vegetable stock

8 cherry tomatoes

salt and freshly ground black pepper

3 tbsp freshly shredded basil

1 Heat the oil in a large saucepan. Add the leek, garlic and oregano and cook gently for 5 minutes, stirring occasionally.

2 Stir in the green beans and the cannellini beans. Sprinkle in the pasta and pour in the stock.

3 Bring the stock mixture to the boil, then reduce the heat to a simmer.

4 Cook for 12–15 minutes or until the vegetables are tender and the pasta is cooked to 'al dente'. Stir occasionally.

5 In a heavy-based frying pan, dry-fry the tomatoes over a high heat until they soften and the skins begin to blacken.

6 Gently crush the tomatoes in the pan with the back of a spoon and add to the soup.

7 Season to taste with salt and pepper. Stir in the shredded basil and serve immediately.

CHEF'S TIP
For an even better taste, make the soup the day before it is to be served and add a little extra stock when reheating.

Lamb & Potato Moussaka

Ingredients
Serves 4

700 g/1½ lb cooked roast lamb

700 g/1½ lb potatoes, peeled

125 g/4 oz butter

1 large onion, peeled and chopped

2–4 garlic cloves, peeled and crushed

3 tbsp tomato purée

1 tbsp freshly chopped parsley

salt and freshly ground black pepper

3–4 tbsp olive oil

2 medium aubergines, trimmed and sliced

4 medium tomatoes, sliced

2 medium eggs

300 ml/½ pint Greek yogurt

2–3 tbsp Parmesan cheese, grated

CHEF'S TIP
To remove any bitterness from the aubergines, layer the slices in a colander with a little salt sprinkled between each one. Leave for 20 minutes, then rinse under cold water. Pat dry on kitchen paper.

1 Preheat the oven to 200°C/ 400°F/Gas Mark 6, about 15 minutes before required. Trim the lamb, discarding any fat then cut into fine dice and reserve. Thinly slice the potatoes and rinse thoroughly in cold water, then pat dry with a clean tea towel.

2 Melt 50 g/2 oz of the butter in a frying pan and fry the potatoes, in batches, until crisp and golden. Using a slotted spoon, remove from the pan and reserve. Use a third of the potatoes to line the base of an ovenproof dish.

3 Add the onion and garlic to the butter remaining in the pan and cook for 5 minutes. Add the lamb and fry for 1 minute. Blend the tomato purée with 3 tablespoons of water and stir into the pan with the parsley and salt and pepper. Spoon over the layer of potatoes, then top with the remaining potato slices.

4 Heat the oil and the remaining butter in the pan and brown the aubergine slices for 5–6 minutes. Arrange the tomatoes on top of the potatoes, then the aubergines on top of the tomatoes. Beat the eggs with the yogurt and Parmesan cheese and pour over the aubergine and tomatoes. Bake in the preheated oven for 25 minutes, or until golden and piping hot. Serve.

Light Ratatouille

Ingredients
Serves 4

1 red pepper
2 courgettes, trimmed
1 small aubergine, trimmed
1 onion, peeled
2 ripe tomatoes
50 g/2 oz button mushrooms, wiped and halved or quartered
200 ml/7 fl oz tomato juice
1 tbsp freshly chopped basil
salt and freshly ground black pepper

1 Deseed the peppers, remove the membrane with a small sharp knife and cut into small dice. Thickly slice the courgettes and cut the aubergine into small dice. Slice the onion into rings.

2 Place the tomatoes in boiling water until their skins begin to peel away.

3 Remove the skins from the tomatoes, cut into quarters and remove the seeds.

4 Place all the vegetables in a saucepan with the tomato juice and basil. Season to taste with salt and pepper.

5 Bring to the boil, cover and simmer for 15 minutes or until the vegetables are tender.

6 Remove the vegetables with a slotted spoon and arrange in a serving dish.

7 Bring the liquid in the pan to the boil and boil for 20 seconds until it is slightly thickened. Season the sauce to taste with salt and pepper.

8 Pass the sauce through a sieve to remove some of the seeds and pour over the vegetables. Serve the ratatouille hot or cold.

Mediterranean Feast

Ingredients
Serves 4

1 small iceberg lettuce
225 g/8 oz French beans
225 g/8 oz baby new
    potatoes, scrubbed
4 medium eggs
1 green pepper
1 medium onion, peeled
200 g can tuna in brine,
    drained and flaked
    into small pieces
50 g/2 oz low-fat hard
    cheese, such as Edam,
    cut into small cubes
8 ripe but firm cherry
    tomatoes, quartered
50 g/2 oz black pitted
    olives, halved
freshly chopped basil,
    to garnish

Lime vinaigrette

3 tbsp light olive oil
2 tbsp white wine
    vinegar
4 tbsp lime juice
grated rind of 1 lime
1 tsp Dijon mustard
1-2 tsp caster sugar
salt and freshly ground
    black pepper

CHEF'S TIP
Cans of tuna now include
varieties such as yellow
fin. Always choose tuna
steaks over chunks.

1 Cut the lettuce into 4 and remove the hard core. Tear into bite-sized pieces and arrange on a large serving platter.

2 Cook the French beans in boiling salted water for 8 minutes and the potatoes for 10 minutes or until tender. Drain and rinse in cold water until cool, then cut both the beans and potatoes in half with a sharp knife.

3 Boil the eggs for 10 minutes, then rinse thoroughly under a cold running tap until cool. Remove the shells under water and cut each egg into four.

4 Remove the seeds from the pepper and cut into thin strips and finely chop the onion.

5 Arrange the beans, potatoes, eggs, peppers and onion on top of the lettuce. Add the tuna, cheese and tomatoes. Sprinkle over the olives and garnish with the basil.

6 To make the vinaigrette, place all the ingredients in a screw-topped jar and shake vigorously until everything is mixed thoroughly. Spoon 4 tablespoons over the top of the prepared salad and serve the remainder separately.

Mediterranean Fish Stew

Ingredients
Serves 4–6

4 tbsp olive oil
1 onion, peeled and
  finely sliced
5 garlic cloves, peeled
  and finely sliced
1 fennel bulb, trimmed
  and finely chopped
3 celery sticks, trimmed
  and finely chopped
400 g can chopped
  tomatoes with Italian
  herbs
1 tbsp freshly chopped
  oregano
1 bay leaf
zest and juice of
  1 orange
1 tsp saffron strands
750 ml/1¼ pints fish
  stock
3 tbsp dry vermouth
salt and freshly ground
  black pepper
225 g/8 oz thick
  haddock fillets
225 g/8 oz sea bass or
  bream fillets
225 g/8 oz raw tiger
  prawns, peeled
crusty bread, to serve

1 Heat the olive oil in a large saucepan. Add the onion, garlic, fennel and celery and cook over a low heat for 15 minutes, stirring frequently until the vegetables are soft and just beginning to turn brown.

2 Add the canned tomatoes with their juice, oregano, bay leaf, orange zest and juice with the saffron strands. Bring to the boil, then reduce the heat and simmer for 5 minutes. Add the fish stock, vermouth and season to taste with salt and pepper. Bring to the boil. Reduce the heat and simmer for 20 minutes.

3 Wipe or rinse the haddock and bass fillets and remove as many of the bones as possible. Place on a chopping board and cut into 5 cm/2 inch cubes. Add to the saucepan and cook for 3 minutes. Add the prawns and cook for a further 5 minutes. Adjust the seasoning to taste and serve with crusty bread.

Mediterranean Potato Salad

Ingredients
Serves 4

700 g/1½ lb small waxy potatoes
2 red onions, peeled and roughly chopped
1 yellow pepper, deseeded and roughly chopped
1 green pepper, deseeded and roughly chopped
6 tbsp extra-virgin olive oil
125 g/4 oz ripe tomatoes, chopped
50 g/2 oz pitted black olives, sliced
125 g/4 oz Feta cheese
3 tbsp freshly chopped parsley
2 tbsp white wine vinegar
1 tsp Dijon mustard
1 tsp clear honey
salt and freshly ground black pepper
sprigs of fresh parsley, to garnish

CHEF'S TIP
When buying tomatoes, look for ones sold still attached to the vine for a particularly rich flavour.

1 Preheat the oven to 200°C/ 400°F/Gas Mark 6. Place the potatoes in a large saucepan of salted water, bring to the boil and simmer until just tender. Do not overcook. Drain and plunge into cold water, to stop them from cooking further.

2 Place the onions in a bowl with the yellow and green peppers, then pour over 2 tablespoons of the olive oil. Stir and spoon onto a large baking tray. Cook in the preheated oven for 25–30 minutes, or until the vegetables are tender and lightly charred in places, stirring occasionally. Remove from the oven and transfer to a large bowl.

3 Cut the potatoes into bite-sized pieces and mix with the roasted onions and peppers. Add the tomatoes and olives to the potatoes. Crumble over the Feta cheese and sprinkle with the chopped parsley.

4 Whisk together the remaining olive oil, vinegar, mustard and honey, then season to taste with salt and pepper. Pour the dressing over the potatoes and toss gently together. Garnish with parsley sprigs and serve immediately.

Mussels Arrabbiata

Ingredients
Serves 4

1.8 kg/4 lb live mussels
3–4 tbsp olive oil
1 large onion, peeled
   and sliced
4 garlic cloves, peeled
   and finely chopped
1 red chilli, deseeded
   and finely chopped
3 x 400 g cans chopped
   tomatoes
150 ml/¼ pint white
   wine
175 g/6 oz black olives,
   pitted and halved
salt and freshly ground
   black pepper
2 tbsp freshly chopped
   parsley
warm crusty bread,
   to serve

1 Clean the mussels by scrubbing with a small, soft brush, removing the beards and any barnacles from the shells. Discard any mussels that are open or have damaged shells. Place in a large bowl and cover with cold water. Change the water frequently before cooking and leave in the refrigerator until required.

2 Heat the olive oil in a large saucepan and sweat the onion, garlic and chilli until soft, but not coloured. Add the tomatoes and bring to the boil, then simmer for 15 minutes.

3 Add the white wine to the tomato sauce, bring the sauce to the boil and add the mussels. Cover and carefully shake the pan. Cook the mussels for 5–7 minutes, or until the shells have opened.

4 Add the olives to the pan and cook uncovered for about 5 minutes to warm through. Season to taste with salt and pepper and sprinkle in the chopped parsley. Discard any mussels that have not opened and serve immediately with lots of warm crusty bread.

CHEF'S TIP
Simmering is essential to bring out the flavours in this sauce. It is also very good with poultry, meat and pasta.

Mussels with Creamy Garlic & Saffron Sauce

Ingredients
Serves 4

700 g/1½ lb live mussels
300 ml/½ pint good-quality dry white wine
1 tbsp olive oil
1 shallot, peeled and finely chopped
2 garlic cloves, peeled and crushed
1 tbsp freshly chopped oregano
2 saffron strands
150 ml/¼ pint single cream
salt and freshly ground black pepper
fresh crusty bread, to serve

CHEF'S TIP
Buy fresh mussels on the day they are to be eaten and place them in cold water in the refrigerator as soon as possible. Change the water at least every two hours.

1 Clean the mussels thoroughly in plenty of cold water and remove any beards and barnacles from the shells. Discard any mussels that are open or damaged. Place in a large bowl and cover with cold water and leave in the refrigerator until required, if prepared earlier.

2 Pour the wine into a large saucepan and bring to the boil. Tip the mussels into the pan, cover and cook, shaking the saucepan periodically for 6–8 minutes, or until the mussels have opened completely.

3 Discard any mussels with closed shells, then using a slotted spoon, carefully remove the remaining open mussels from the saucepan and keep them warm. Reserve the cooking liquor.

4 Heat the olive oil in a small frying pan and cook the shallot and garlic gently for 2–3 minutes, until softened. Add the reserved cooking liquid and chopped oregano and cook for a further 3–4 minutes. Stir in the saffron and the cream and heat through gently. Season to taste with salt and pepper. Place a few mussels in individual serving bowls and spoon over the saffron sauce. Serve immediately with plenty of fresh crusty bread.

Ossobuco with Saffron Risotto

Ingredients
Serves 4

125 g/4 oz butter
2 tbsp olive oil
4 large pieces of shin of veal (often sold as ossobuco)
2 onions, peeled and roughly chopped
2 garlic cloves, peeled and finely chopped
300 ml/½ pint white wine
5 plum tomatoes, peeled and chopped
1 tbsp tomato purée
salt and freshly ground black pepper
2 tbsp freshly chopped parsley
grated rind of 1 small lemon
few strands of saffron, crushed
350 g/12 oz Arborio rice
1.3 litres/2¼ pints chicken stock, heated
50 g/2 oz Parmesan cheese, grated

1 Heat 50 g/2 oz butter with half the oil in a large saucepan and add the pieces of veal. Brown lightly on both sides, then transfer to a plate. Add half the onion and garlic and cook gently for about 10 minutes until the onion is just golden.

2 Return the veal to the saucepan along with the white wine, tomatoes and tomato purée. Season lightly with salt and pepper, cover and bring to a gentle simmer. Cook very gently for 1 hour. Uncover and cook for a further 30 minutes until the meat is cooked and the sauce is reduced and thickened. Season to taste. Mix together the remaining garlic, parsley and lemon rind and reserve.

3 Meanwhile, slowly melt the remaining butter and oil in a large, deep-sided frying pan. Add the remaining onion and cook gently for 5–7 minutes until just brown. Add the saffron and stir for a few seconds, then add the rice. Cook for a further minute until the rice is well coated in oil and butter.

5 Begin adding the stock a ladleful at a time, stirring well after each addition of stock and waiting until it is absorbed before adding the next. Continue in this way until all the stock is used. Remove from the heat and stir in the grated Parmesan cheese and seasoning.

6 Spoon a little of the saffron risotto onto each of four serving plates. Top with the ossobuco and sauce and sprinkle over the reserved garlic and parsley mixture. Serve immediately.

Paella

Ingredients
Serves 6

450 g/1 lb live mussels
4 tbsp olive oil
6 medium chicken
  thighs
1 medium onion, peeled
  and finely chopped
1 garlic clove, peeled
  and crushed
225 g/8 oz tomatoes,
  skinned, deseeded
  and chopped
1 red pepper, deseeded
  and chopped
1 green pepper, deseeded
  and chopped
125 g/4 oz frozen peas
1 tsp paprika
450 g/1 lb Arborio rice
½ tsp turmeric
900 ml/1½ pints chicken
  stock, warmed
175 g/6 oz large peeled
  prawns
salt and freshly ground
  black pepper
2 limes
1 lemon
1 tbsp freshly chopped
  basil
whole cooked unpeeled
  prawns, to garnish

1 Rinse the mussels under cold running water, scrubbing well to remove any grit and barnacles, then pull off the hairy 'beards'. Tap any open mussels sharply with a knife, and discard if they refuse to close.

2 Heat the oil in a paella pan or large, heavy-based frying pan and cook the chicken thighs for 10–15 minutes until golden. Remove and keep warm.

3 Fry the onion and garlic in the remaining oil in the pan for 2–3 minutes, then add the tomatoes, peppers, peas and paprika and cook for a further 3 minutes.

4 Add the rice to the pan and return the chicken with the turmeric and half the stock. Bring to the boil and simmer, gradually adding more stock as it is absorbed. Cook for 20 minutes, or until most of the stock has been absorbed and the rice is almost tender.

5 Put the mussels in a large saucepan with 5 cm/2 inches boiling salted water, cover and steam for 5 minutes. Discard any with shells that have not opened, then stir into the rice with the prawns. Season to taste with salt and pepper. Heat through for 2–3 minutes until piping hot. Squeeze the juice from one of the limes over the paella.

6 Cut the remaining limes and the lemon into wedges and arrange on top of the paella. Sprinkle with the basil, garnish with the prawns and serve.

Peperonata

Ingredients
Serves 6

2 red peppers
2 yellow peppers
450 g/1 lb waxy
    potatoes
1 large onion
2 tbsp good-quality
    virgin olive oil
700 g/1½ lb tomatoes,
    peeled, deseeded and
    chopped
2 small courgettes
50 g/2 oz pitted black
    olives, quartered
small handful basil
    leaves
salt and freshly ground
    black pepper
crusty bread, to serve

1 Prepare the peppers by halving them lengthwise and removing the stems, seeds, and membranes.

2 Cut the peppers lengthwise into strips about 1 cm/½ inch wide. Peel the potatoes and cut into rough dice, about 2.5–3 cm/1–1¼ inch across. Cut the onion lengthwise into eight wedges.

3 Heat the olive oil in a large saucepan over a medium heat.

4 Add the onion and cook for about 5 minutes, or until starting to brown.

5 Add the peppers, potatoes, tomatoes, courgettes, black olives and about four torn basil leaves. Season to taste with salt and pepper.

6 Stir the mixture, cover and cook over a very low heat for about 40 minutes, or until the vegetables are tender but still hold their shape. Garnish with the remaining basil. Transfer to a serving bowl and serve immediately, with chunks of crusty bread.

CHEF'S TIP
Chunks of baguette, as shown in the picture, would work well with this recipe but you could also use freshly baked ciabatta or foccaccia, which would add an extra taste of the Mediterranean.

Roasted Red Pepper, Tomato & Red Onion Soup

Ingredients
Serves 4

fine spray of oil
2 large red peppers,
    deseeded and roughly
    chopped
1 red onion, peeled and
    roughly chopped
350 g/12 oz tomatoes,
    halved
1 small crusty French
    loaf
1 garlic clove, peeled
600 ml/1 pint vegetable
    stock
salt and freshly ground
    black pepper
1 tsp Worcestershire
    sauce
4 tbsp half-fat fromage
    frais

1 Preheat the oven to 190°C/ 375°F/Gas Mark 5. Spray a large roasting tin with the oil and place the peppers and onion in the base. Cook in the oven for 10 minutes. Add the tomatoes and cook for a further 20 minutes or until the peppers are soft.

2 Cut the bread into 1 cm/½ inch slices. Cut the garlic clove in half and rub the cut edge of the garlic over the bread.

3 Place all the bread slices on a large baking tray, and bake in the preheated oven for 10 minutes, turning halfway through, until golden and crisp.

4 Remove the vegetables from the oven and allow to cool slightly, then blend in a food processor until smooth. Strain the vegetable mixture through a large nylon sieve into a saucepan, to remove the seeds and skin. Add the stock, season to taste with salt and pepper and stir to mix. Heat the soup gently until piping hot.

5 In a small bowl beat together the Worcestershire sauce with the fromage frais.

6 Pour the soup into warmed bowls and swirl a spoonful of the fromage frais mixture into each bowl. Serve immediately with the garlic toasts.

Roasted Cod with Saffron Aïoli

Ingredients

Serves 4

For the saffron Aïoli

2 garlic cloves, peeled
¼ tsp saffron strands
sea salt, to taste
1 medium egg yolk
200 ml/7 fl oz extra-
    virgin olive oil
2 tbsp lemon juice

For the marinade

2 tbsp olive oil
4 garlic cloves, peeled
    and finely chopped
1 red onion, peeled and
    finely chopped
1 tbsp freshly chopped
    rosemary
2 tbsp freshly chopped
    thyme

4–6 sprigs of fresh
    rosemary
1 lemon, sliced
4 x 175 g/6 oz thick cod
    fillets with skin
freshly cooked
    vegetables, to serve

1 Preheat oven to 180°C/ 350°F/Gas Mark 4 10 minutes before cooking. Crush the garlic, saffron and a pinch of salt in a pestle and mortar to form a paste. Place in a blender with the egg yolk and blend for 30 seconds. With the motor running, slowly add the olive oil in a thin, steady stream until the mayonnaise is smooth and thick. Spoon into a small bowl and stir in the lemon juice. Cover and leave in the refrigerator until required.

2 Combine the olive oil, garlic, red onion, rosemary and thyme for the marinade and leave to infuse for about 10 minutes.

3 Place the sprigs of rosemary and slices of lemon in the bottom of a lightly oiled roasting tin. Add the cod, skin-side up. Pour over the prepared marinade and leave to marinate in the refrigerator for 15–20 minutes. Bake in the preheated oven for 15–20 minutes, or until the cod is cooked and the flesh flakes easily with a fork. Leave the cod to rest for 1 minute before serving with the saffron aïoli and vegetables.

Roasted Aubergine Dip with Pitta Strips

Ingredients
Serves 4

4 pitta breads
2 large aubergines
1 garlic clove, peeled
¼ tsp sesame oil
1 tbsp lemon juice
½ tsp ground cumin
salt and freshly ground
  black pepper
2 tbsp freshly chopped
  parsley
fresh salad leaves,
  to serve

1 Preheat the oven to 180°C/ 350°F/Gas Mark 4. On a chopping board cut the pitta breads into strips. Spread the bread in a single layer onto a large baking tray.

2 Cook in the preheated oven for 15 minutes until golden and crisp. Leave to cool on a wire cooling rack.

3 Trim the aubergines, rinse lightly and reserve. Heat a griddle pan until almost smoking. Cook the aubergines and garlic for about 15 minutes.

4 Turn the aubergines frequently, until very tender with wrinkled and charred skins. Remove from heat. Leave to cool.

5 When the aubergines are cool enough to handle, cut in half and scoop out the cooked flesh and place in a food processor.

6 Squeeze the softened garlic flesh from the papery skin and add to the aubergine.

7 Blend the aubergine and garlic until smooth, then add the sesame oil, lemon juice and cumin and blend again to mix.

8 Season to taste with salt and pepper, stir in the parsley and serve with the pitta strips and mixed salad leaves.

Sicilian Baked Aubergine

Ingredients
Serves 4

1 large aubergine,
    trimmed
2 celery stalks, trimmed
4 large ripe tomatoes
1 tsp sunflower oil
2 shallots, peeled and
    finely chopped
1½ tsp tomato purée
25 g/1 oz green pitted
    olives
25 g/1 oz black pitted
    olives
salt and freshly ground
    black pepper
1 tbsp white wine
    vinegar
2 tsp caster sugar
1 tbsp freshly chopped
    basil, to garnish
mixed salad leaves,
    to serve

1 Preheat the oven to 200°C/ 400°F/Gas Mark 6. Cut the aubergine into small cubes and place on an oiled baking tray.

2 Cover the tray with tinfoil and bake in the preheated oven for 15–20 minutes until soft. Reserve, to allow the aubergine to cool.

3 Place the celery and tomatoes in a large bowl and cover with boiling water.

4 Remove the tomatoes from the bowl when their skins begin to peel away. Remove the skins then, deseed and chop the flesh into small pieces.

5 Remove the celery from the bowl of water, finely chop and reserve.

6 Pour the sunflower oil into a non-stick saucepan, add the chopped shallots and fry gently for 2–3 minutes until soft. Add the celery, tomatoes, tomato purée and olives. Season to taste with salt and pepper.

7 Simmer gently for 3–4 minutes. Add the vinegar, sugar and cooled aubergine to the pan and heat gently for 2–3 minutes until all the ingredients are well blended. Reserve to allow the aubergine mixture to cool. When cool, garnish with the chopped basil and serve cold with salad leaves.

Spanish Omelette with Smoked Cod

Ingredients
Serves 3–4

3 tbsp sunflower oil

350 g/12 oz potatoes, peeled and cut into 1 cm/½ inch cubes

2 medium onions, peeled and cut into wedges

2–4 large garlic cloves, peeled and thinly sliced

1 large red pepper, deseeded, quartered and thinly sliced

125 g/4 oz smoked cod

salt and freshly ground black pepper

25 g/1 oz butter, melted

1 tbsp double cream

6 medium eggs, beaten

2 tbsp freshly chopped flat-leaf parsley

50 g/2 oz mature Cheddar cheese, grated

To serve

crusty bread

tossed green salad

1 Heat the oil in a large non-stick heavy-based frying pan, add the potatoes, onions and garlic and cook gently for 10–15 minutes until golden brown, then add the red pepper and cook for 3 minutes.

2 Meanwhile, place the fish in a shallow frying pan and cover with water. Season to taste with salt and pepper and poach gently for 10 minutes. Drain and flake the fish into a bowl, toss in the melted butter and cream, adjust the seasoning and reserve.

3 When the vegetables are cooked, drain off any excess oil and stir in the beaten egg with the chopped parsley. Pour the fish mixture over the top and cook gently for 5 minutes, or until the eggs become firm.

4 Sprinkle the grated cheese over the top and place the pan under a preheated hot grill. Cook for 2–3 minutes until the cheese is golden and bubbling. Carefully slide the omelette onto a large plate and serve immediately with plenty of bread and salad.

Spanish-style Pork Stew with Saffron Rice

Ingredients
Serves 4

2 tbsp olive oil
900 g/2 lb boneless
  pork shoulder, diced
1 large onion, peeled
  and sliced
2 garlic cloves, peeled
  and finely chopped
1 tbsp plain flour
450 g/1 lb plum
  tomatoes, peeled and
  chopped
175 ml/6 fl oz red wine
1 tbsp freshly chopped
  basil
1 green pepper,
  deseeded and sliced
50 g/2 oz pimiento-
  stuffed olives, cut in
  half crossways
salt and freshly ground
  black pepper
fresh basil leaves, to
  garnish

For the saffron rice

1 tbsp olive oil
25 g/1 oz butter
1 small onion, peeled
  and finely chopped
few strands of saffron,
  crushed
250 g/9 oz long-grain
  white rice
600 ml/1 pint chicken
  stock

1 Preheat the oven to 150°C/ 300°F/Gas Mark 2. Heat the oil in a large flameproof casserole and add the pork in batches. Fry over a high heat until browned. Transfer to a plate until all the pork is browned.

2 Lower the heat and add the onion to the casserole. Cook for a further 5 minutes until soft and starting to brown. Add the garlic and stir briefly before returning the pork to the casserole. Add the flour and stir.

3 Add the tomatoes. Gradually stir in the red wine and add the basil. Bring to simmering point and cover. Transfer the casserole to the lower part of the preheated oven and cook for 1½ hours. Stir in the green pepper and olives and cook for 30 minutes. Season to taste with salt and pepper.

4 Meanwhile, to make the saffron rice, heat the oil with the butter in a saucepan. Add the onion and cook for 5 minutes over a medium heat until softened. Add the saffron and rice and stir well. Add the stock, bring to the boil, cover and reduce the heat as low as possible. Cook for 15 minutes, covered, until the rice is tender and the stock is absorbed. Adjust the seasoning and serve with the stew, garnished with fresh basil.

Tomato & Basil Soup

Ingredients
Serves 4

1.1 kg/2½ lb ripe
   tomatoes, cut in half
2 garlic cloves
1 tsp olive oil
1 tbsp balsamic vinegar
1 tbsp dark brown
   sugar
1 tbsp tomato purée
300 ml/½ pint
   vegetable stock
6 tbsp low-fat natural
   yogurt
2 tbsp freshly chopped
   basil
salt and freshly ground
   black pepper
small basil leaves,
   to garnish

1 Preheat the oven to 200°C/ 400°F/Gas Mark 6. Evenly spread the tomatoes and unpeeled garlic in a single layer in a large roasting tin.

2 Mix the oil and vinegar together. Drizzle over the tomatoes and sprinkle with the dark brown sugar.

3 Roast the tomatoes in the preheated oven for 20 minutes until tender and lightly charred in places.

4 Remove from the oven and allow to cool slightly. When cool enough to handle, squeeze the softened flesh of the garlic from the papery skin. Place with the charred tomatoes in a nylon sieve over a saucepan.

5 Press the garlic and tomato through the sieve with the back of a wooden spoon.

6 When all the flesh has been sieved, add the tomato purée and vegetable stock to the pan. Heat gently, stirring occasionally.

7 In a small bowl beat the yogurt and basil together and season to taste with salt and pepper. Stir the basil yogurt into the soup. Garnish with basil leaves and serve immediately.

CHEF'S TIP
Use the sweetest type of tomatoes available as it makes a big difference to the taste of the soup.

Chargrilled Vegetable & Goats' Cheese Pizza

Ingredients
Serves 4

125 g/4 oz baking potato
1 tbsp olive oil
225 g/8 oz strong white flour
½ tsp salt
1 tsp easy-blend dried yeast

For the topping

1 medium aubergine, thinly sliced
2 small courgettes, trimmed and sliced lengthways
1 yellow pepper, quartered and deseeded
1 red onion, peeled and sliced into very thin wedges
5 tbsp olive oil
175 g/6 oz cooked new potatoes, halved
400 g can chopped tomatoes, drained
2 tsp freshly chopped oregano
125 g/4 oz Mozzarella cheese, cut into small cubes
125 g/4 oz goats' cheese, crumbled

1 Preheat the oven to 220°C/ 425°F/Gas Mark 7 15 minutes before baking. Put a baking sheet in the oven to heat up. Cook the potato in lightly salted boiling water until tender. Peel and mash with the olive oil until smooth.

2 Sift the flour and salt into a bowl. Stir in the yeast. Add the mashed potato and 150 ml/¼ pint warm water and mix to a soft dough. Knead for 5–6 minutes, until smooth. Put the dough in a bowl, cover with clingfilm and leave to rise in a warm place for 30 minutes.

3 To make the topping, arrange the aubergine, courgettes, pepper and onion, skin-side up, on a grill rack and brush with 4 tablespoons of the oil. Grill for 4–5 minutes. Turn the vegetables and brush with the remaining oil. Grill for 3–4 minutes. Cool, skin and slice the pepper. Put all of the vegetables in a bowl, add the halved new potatoes and toss gently together. Set aside.

4 Briefly re-knead the dough then roll out to a 30.5–35.5 cm/12–14 inch round, according to preferred thickness. Mix the tomatoes and oregano together and spread over the pizza base. Scatter over the Mozzarella cheese. Put the pizza on the preheated baking sheet and bake for 8 minutes.

5 Arrange the vegetables and goats' cheese on top and bake for 8–10 minutes. Serve.

This is a Star Fire book
First Published in 2003

02 04 05 03 01

1 3 5 7 9 10 8 6 4 2

Star Fire is part of The Foundry Creative Media Company Limited
Crabtree Hall, Crabtree Lane, Fulham, London, SW6 6TY
Visit the Foundry website: www.foundry.co.uk

visit our cookery website: www.practicalrecipes.com

ISBN: 1-904041-06-X

The CIP record for this book is available from the British Library

Printed in Croatia

ACKNOWLEDGEMENTS

Authors: Catherine Atkinson, Juliet Barker, Liz Martin,
Gina Steer, Carol Tennant, Mari Mereid Williams,
Elizabeth Wolf-Cohen, Simone Wright

Editorial Consultant: Gina Steer

Editors: Michelle Clare, Karen Fitzpatrick, Vicky Garrard, Julia Rolf
Photography: Colin Bowling and Paul Forrester

Home Economists and Stylists: Jacqueline Bellefontaine,
Mandy Phipps, Vicki Smallwood and Penny Stephens

Design Team: Helen Courtney, Jennifer Bishop,
Lucy Bradbury and Chris Herbert

All props supplied by Barbara Stewart at Surfaces

NOTE

Recipes using uncooked eggs should be avoided by infants, the
elderly, pregnant women and anyone suffering from an illness.